CHOPPERS

FIELD GUIDE

Doug Mitchel

CUSTOM BIKES 1950s-PRESENT

©2004 by KP Books

Published by

kp **kp books**
An imprint of F+W Publications, Inc.

700 East State Street • Iola, WI 54990-0001
715-445-2214 • 888-457-2873

Our toll-free number to place an order or obtain a free catalog is (800) 258-0929.

Library of Congress Catalog Number: 2004113678
ISBN: 0-87349-964-6

Designed by: Wendy Wendt
Edited by: Brian Earnest
Printed in United States of America

CONTENTS

CONTENTS

To Lou and Mary Mazzone,
for the inspiration
and the metal flake

ACKNOWLEDGMENTS

I need to thank all the owners of the amazing machines that are included in this work. Special thanks goes out to the shops that went the extra mile to make my life easier, and this book more interesting:

Crown Custom Cycle Fabrication, Park City, Illinois
Custom Shop Cycles, Flanagan, Illinois
DD Custom Cycles, Gurnee, Illinois
Ideal Ride Custom Motorcycle Emporium, East Dundee, Illinois
J&P Cycles, Anamosa, Iowa
Johnny Legend Customs, Wheaton, Illinois
National Motorcycle Museum, Anamosa, Iowa
Prison City Choppers, Joliet, Illinois
Sound F/X Motorcycle Engineering, Elmwood Park, Illinois
Suicycles, Rockdale, Illinois
Uke's Harley-Davidson, Kenosha, Wisconsin
Windwalkers Motorcycles of Naperville, Illinois
X-Treme Cycle Tech, Aurora, Illinois

The birth of the chopper can be loosely traced to the late 1940s, when soldiers returning from World War II found a few dollars in their uniforms, and surplus military motorcycles for sale. Once the purchase was made, any excess hardware was chopped off, thus creating the slang term "chopper" for such a machine. The "bobber" style had been around for a bit longer as machines used on the racetracks were seen wearing bobbed rear fenders. These home-built machines were often ridden to the race, put onto the track, then ridden home again. They needed to retain some level of legality, although laws were a bit more lax then.

In the latter part of the 1960s, owners and builders sought ways to enhance their chopped-down bikes with something more. There is no way of knowing who the first person was to add length to the front forks to change the riding characteristics as well as the appearance of their scoot. Sonny Barger of Hell's Angels fame was perhaps the first person of notoriety to do so, but he may not have been the first to make the change.

Over the years, the art of customizing motorcycles transcended into something more than the owner welding on a few doo-dads and riding into history. By the time the 1990s were coming to a close, building choppers had become big business. Many of the well-known names were soon behind the handlebars of small empires, not just a small business running out of a suburban garage. Of course, there were magazines catering to the chopper fan for many years, but by the early 2000s the small screen was being inundated with weekly episodes of big-dollar builders wielding their welding torches and spray guns.

This book attempts to encompass many levels of choppers being built and ridden today. Some of the machines you see have been around for decades, while others are brand-new examples of the finest technology money can buy. Regardless of the ones you like the best, they were all created with the builders with passion and talent. As many will tell you, there's no easy way to build a chopper, but some builders just make it look that way.

(At right:) America was not the only place the chopper revolution was happening. In France, a man by the name of Maurice Combalbert is considered to be the premier builder of choppers. Brigitte Bardot was mounted astride one of his creations when she sang "Harley-Davidson" in one of her films. Maurice's early days were spent working in a retail operation that sold motorcycles and furniture. Harley-Davidson, Triumph and Norton motorcycles could be purchased along with coffee tables and bedroom sets. Combalbert choppers remain among the most coveted items with French motorcycle fans.

courtesy of Charlie Lecach

THE HOBO

Aptly named "The Hobo," this machine was the result of many years of collecting bits and pieces from events around the country. The parts and frame were amassed during a 3-year period before construction began. Ninety percent of the bike is hand fabricated, and the details are abundant. A jet-ski throttle and hand grips off of a Schwinn are among the tiny bits that make up a truly custom chopper.

Owner: Dan Cheeseman/Klock Werks

The Panhead mill has been modified extensively, and now measures 88 cubic inches in displacement. The exhaust tubes are hand built, and part of the long list of components created by the team at Klock Werks.

The Moon Eyes fuel tank is capped by a three-spoke, wheel knock-off borrowed from a European auto, and the hand shift once resided in a corner pub. There are no limits to the creativity utilized in the creation of this mount.

The stock frame has been heavily modified, including the addition of the curvaceous "devil's horns" found on the front downtube. House of Kolor Gold Flake paint is used to finish the frame, and is highlighted by contrasting scallops.

PRO-ONE ONE-OFF

Based on a Pro-One frame, almost every inch of this pro-street chopper has been hand built. Only 2 months were required to do the complete build. The finished machine is being raffled off to benefit a charity organization, and the winner will get a lot of machine for the small cost of a ticket.

Owner: Custom Shop Cycles

All of the sheet metal on the bike has been hand crafted, including the svelte and sensual fairing. A wire form was used to create the general shape, then the remaining form was built up to create the final component.

The 100-cubic-inch Rev Tech motor is surrounded by a sea of custom body panels. The shapely chin fairing leads the way and helps to keep the airflow smooth as the rider takes to the open road. The screened portion of the piece keeps bugs and debris from reaching the engine while allowing plenty of cooling air through the mesh. The vent seen on the fuel tank is only painted on, and is one of many illusions found on the elaborate color scheme.

The rear suspension duties are handled by a Pro-One four-link system that keeps the rear wheel firmly planted while allowing for a high level of comfort. The solid rear wheel is provided by Turbine, and contrasts nicely with the spoked Turbine wheel used up front. HHI brakes are used on both wheels.

TRIUMPH CUSTOM

Not all choppers were based on Milwaukee iron, as evidenced by this Triumph-powered example. A 1968 Bonneville was the original model before extensive modifications were applied. The frame has remained stock, except the rear shocks were removed and the frame was welded into a rigid member.

Owner: Matthew Tomas

The twin-cylinder power plant displaces 650cc, just as it did when delivered from the factory. Both exhaust pipes have been "bobbed" and extend just beyond the dimension of the motor itself.

The "peanut" fuel tank has been painted in a popular flame scheme to mimic a design the owner saw on another chopper. The quadruple spike fuel cap reminds us that this machine was built when old school was new. The owner found this cycle in Chicago and restored it to its current condition.

Another feature often used on older choppers were the spiked axle caps. The 21-inch front spoked wheel rolls without the benefit of a brake of any kind. The 16-inch rear wheel was fitted with a simple drum brake to slow the bike.

ATLAS HARD TAIL

Panhead-powered choppers were a common sight in the 1950s and 1960s, and remain a popular choice today. This Atlas hard tail-framed example is motivated by a 74-cubic-inch mill first built in 1958. The setup steers with a girder fork and slows with the help of a trio of Performance Machine rotors.

Owner: Michael Bailey

The straight-pipe exhaust was hand made by the owner, and ensures that no one misses his arrival. A Performance Machine wheel is wrapped with Metzeler rubber in back and provides a confident footprint.

The Panhead motor draws breath through a healthy SU carburetor and a nearly unrestricted velocity stack and filter. A layer of chrome plating completes the package.

The small fuel tank does not permit long hauls on the open road. The chameleon paint fades from blue to red. A contemporary Harley-Davidson logo appears on both sides of the reservoir.

CUSTOM SHOP CYCLES ORIGINAL

It doesn't matter what angle you choose to view this monster, there's something hand built at every point. From the massive 280 series Metzeler rear tire, to the custom sheet metal and frame work, no shortcuts were taken in the fabrication of this supercharged beast.

Owner: Custom Shop Cycles/John Wargo

A frame from Paramount Cycles was heavily modified to accept the supercharged motor, 280 rear tire and front fork from Pro-One. The backbone of the chassis was stretched 6 inches and was then wrapped with bodywork that was created completely from scratch.

The motor has been boosted to displace 113 cubic inches and is force fed by a supercharger mounted to the front of the power plant. Nitrous oxide adds yet another level of punch, delivering a total horsepower rating in the neighborhood of 250. An S&S Super G carburetor manages the flow of fuel and air.

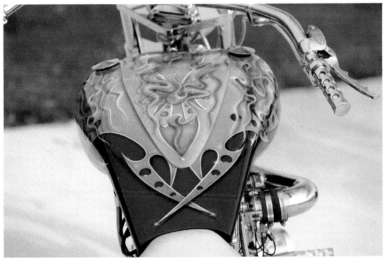

The complex multi-layered color scheme was created and applied by the owner, and subtle applications of the female form can be found in several locations. By producing the entire machine by hand, the owner has shown the world what a motivated builder is capable of.

BARGAIN BEAUTY

Built in only 29 days, this machine was assembled for the budget-minded buyer. No corners were cut, but components, paint and motor mods were kept simple to achieve the desired results.

Owner: Custom Shop Cycles

An 18-inch Sturgis rim is covered with a Metzeler 200 series tire. A large HHI disc brake and caliper are on duty to slow the 100-cubic-inch motor bike down. A rigid frame stays consistent with the majority of today's modern choppers.

Like the rest of this "bargain" model, the sheet metal is coated in copper-pearl paint, complete with ghost flames. A tiny electronic gauge resides just above the flush-mounted fuel cap, keeping the overall appearance neat and tidy.

To complement the copper pearl paint, the two-person saddle has been swaddled in a shade of brown lizard pelt. Although this chopper was built on a budget, it measures up nicely to higher-dollar machines.

MYSTERY '59

Taking the stretched-fork scenario to the limit, this 1959 Panhead doesn't offer much in the way of comfort, but has loads of "wow." The elongated front forks were created by John Harmon, and feature a mysterious set of internal springs. How the setup works remains a secret.

Owner: Steve and Dawn Burr

One end of the internal springs terminate at the front hub, but there is no way to determine how the spring is mounted to the inside of the fork tubes. The designer has passed away, taking his secret with him.

At both ends of the extended tubes that create the forks, the components are welded together with these obvious, yet well-done joints. Overall stiffness is questionable, but the flex provides a modicum of suspension to the otherwise rigid frame.

Devoid of the typical handlebar risers, this 1950s build has the fork tubes welded directly to the triple-trees for support. The peanut tank forces frequent stops for fuel, but lacking in any creature comforts, the rider and passenger probably welcome the chance to dismount.

HARLEY THROWBACK

Based on a 1978 Harley-Davidson FXE, this Shovelhead-powered machine harkens back to the days of bell bottoms and home-built rides. The cases remain stock, but are filled with performance upgrades from S&S and Andrews.

Owner: Terry Douglas

The frame cradling the FXE motor was dipped in cherry paint and trimmed with loads of embellishments. The short exhaust pipes are courtesy of Paughco, and do little to keep things quiet.

Unlike many choppers, this example rides with rear suspension. The chrome shocks are mounted to the swingarm that is also adorned with pinstripes and other decorative trim. The rear brake was standard issue on the FXE for 1978.

A small leather tool bag resides atop the headlight, and is trimmed in the same natural leather as the king-and-queen saddle. Excess baggage was usually not an issue as most riders kept things simple when they took to the open roads.

1930'S HARLEY BOBBER

Assuming The Motor Company ever decided to build a "bobber" model, this is probably what would have rolled out of the factory. Built using a 1931 VL frame that was stretched to hold the 1939 Knucklehead motor, this home-built special really looks the part of the board tracker it is meant to mimic.

Owner: Gene Williams

Only the suicide shifter and springer front end give away the fact that this wasn't a board track racer. The dual chain drive, fenderless front tire and tiny saddle were all seen on the wooden tracks of the 1920s.

The 61-cubic-inch motor is coupled to a 1931 VL transmission and exhales through two exhaust pipes of different lengths. The mill uses a pair of carburetors, each tuned to match the length of pipe it served.

"TANGERINE EXTREME"

"Tangerine Extreme" features a multitude of custom components to create a one-of-a-kind ride. The single-downtube frame is mated to an inverted fork for control and stability. A pair of custom-made wheels also help to set this bike apart from the rest.

Owner: Michael DeWitte

The tear-drop tank is painted in Candy Tangerine and finished off with contrasting ghost flames. The risers bring the handlebars back to the rider's grasp for a comfortable stance.

The Candy Tangerine and ghost flame paint continues on all the sheet metal, including the oil tank. Braided, stainless-steel oil lines keep things neat and help prevent ruptured lines.

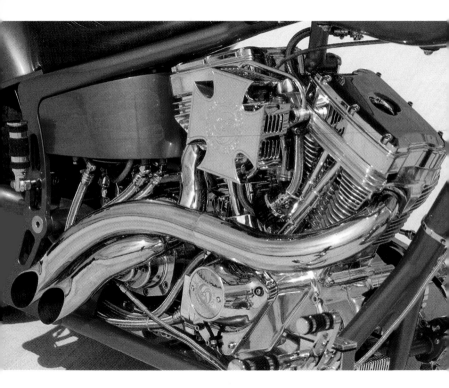

The V-twin motor's capacity has been enlarged to 113 cubic inches, and the cam and cylinder heads are produced by Midwest Chopper. Twisted Sister exhaust tubes give the spent gases a way out.

OLD-SCHOOL SURVIVOR

The chopper shown here has been owned by one man for 35 years. Its current state is the sixth variation since he first bought it. Two years after he rode it home it was wrecked, only to be rebuilt again. It looks "old school" because it is. From the coffin tank to the steel wheels, there's nothing modern about it.

Owner: Jerry Morgan

The coffin fuel tank wears a new coat of modern chameleon paint, but retains its original form. The rigid frame and rear fender also share the color-shifting finish. The paint was also applied by the owner.

The 74-cubic-inch Panhead motor draws breath through this two-barrel Weber carburetor, and runs with 9-to-1 compression pistons. Joe Hunt ignition provides the spark, and Joe Alphabet lets the engine exhale.

Steel wheels from Invader roll at both ends of this time machine, and anyone old enough to remember knows these wheels were THE way to go in the 1960s when building a chopper. Similar offerings are sold today, but they are typically formed from a lighter alloy.

SPENCER II CHOPPERS ORIGINAL

Tired of seeing all the same tanks and fenders on other choppers, the owner of this bike decided to bend up some of his own. The result is certainly one of a kind and award winning. More than 5 months were required to do the work, and the results are indicative of the time taken.

Owner: Spencer II Choppers

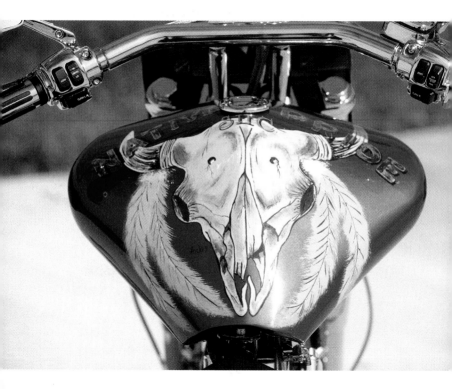

The gracefully shaped fuel tank is only one of the hand-crafted pieces on the chopper. The wide, flowing top panel makes a perfect home for the Southwestern skull graphics.

Continuing the hand-built theme, the rear fender and sissy bar have also been shaped from sheet metal and steel to meet with the owner's specific needs. The light and dark metallic blue paint really shows off the curves and lines of the metal beneath.

The Wide Glide forks hold a rolling wheel from Sturgis and another hand-bent piece that makes up the front fender.

ALL-CUSTOM PANHEAD

The builder of this machine took over 5 years to collect parts before beginning assembly. He knew from the start the kind of chopper he wanted, then took the time to locate all the components required to make it happen. Based on a 1960 Panhead, there is little, if anything, that is stock on the cycle now.

Owner: Darwin Funk

The original motor has been increased in size to displace 92 cubic inches and was built using bits from several vendors. A crank from a Harley Shovelhead throws the bigger pistons through the cylinders, and an Andrews cam is on duty to handle the valve train.

The springer front fork is borrowed from a 1948 Panhead and is considered to be a fairly rare commodity. 1948 was the last year before the newer Hydra-Glide models were introduced, giving new bike buyers the option of sprung or hydraulic forks. The layer of chrome was not a factory option.

In typical chopper fashion the rear end is devoid of any suspension, creating a "hard tail" frame. The rear disc was requisitioned from a 1980 Harley-Davidson Low Rider, and helps to bring this handmade special to a halt.

BUELL LOW-RIDER

Wanting something different than the "typical" long-fork chopper, the owner decided to use a performance model from Buell as the basis for his project. The 1200cc motor has been squeezed into a frame that claims a 32-degree rake, and gives the bike a long, low look. Perhaps more of a bobber than a chopper, it still brings back memories of the early days of building your own ride.

Owner: John Dawson

The Buell motor has been modified for use in this craft with a variety of new hardware. An Andrews cam spins inside, and the cylinder heads are from Thunder Storm. Black heat wrap tape keeps the riders legs safe from burns as the hot gases leave the shortened exhaust tubes.

A pair of cat's eye lenses reside within the small fairing imported from Germany. It may not provide a lot of protection from the elements, but certainly adds a healthy dose of attitude to the overall appearance.

Unlike many choppers being ridden today, this monster is slowed by a huge front rotor that is grabbed by a multi-puck caliper. These pieces are also taken from a factory Buell offering. Combined with the width of the front tire, braking times are as dramatic as the launches.

CUSTOM BAD BOY

The Harley-Davidson Bad Boy was sold in a basic Bobber configuration from your local dealer, but some people just can't leave good enough alone. Applying its vast talents in fabrication and paint, Custom Shop Cycles did its best to turn this Bad Boy into something better.

Owner: Custom Shop Cycles

A 95-cubic-inch motor turns the 200 series rear tire, and Inferno wheels are used at both ends. Performance Machine brakes on both wheels bring the Bad Boy down from speed. Black base paint has been covered with orange and yellow flames, which are highlighted by barbed wire wrapping.

INLINE BOBBER

Not being the kind of man who heeds warnings from others, the owner decided to build himself a bobber that would be confused with no other. With a fuel tank created from three separate tanks, a rear fender off a Triumph and a tail light that's actually a Harley turn signal, you might be fooled several times while trying to identify the origin of this one-off cycle.

Owner: Gene Williams

Just to complicate things further, an inline, four-cylinder motor was chosen for the power plant. Displacing 45 cubic inches, the mill comes from Continental, and was used in industrial equipment. The exhaust was also created by the owner to provide adequate breathing for the four cylinders.

About the only thing typical about this model is the lack of rear suspension. A disc brake from a Shovelhead slows the bike from the rear, while another style taken from a 1941 model is applied to the front wheel.

AGAN ORIGINAL

This creation is the owner's first effort at building a two-wheeled hot rod. The flat black finish and rear whitewall tire provide clues as to the owner's intentions. A Kraft Tech frame is mated to a Wide-Glide front fork, and wire wheels are enveloped with Avon rubber. The 1340cc engine has been massaged to provide an extra measure of motivation as well.

Owner: Mike Agan

Sampson 2 1/2-inch-diameter exhaust pipes have been shortened for faster exit of the gases. The heat wrap tape keeps things cool while protecting uncovered legs from burns. The bobbed rear fender covers only a portion of the rear tire, but helps keep the rider's back dry on wet roads.

The S&S Super E carburetor draws it elixir from this peanut fuel tank mounted to the frame. Only capable of holding 2.5 gallons, it gives the rider plenty of reasons to keep his travels close to home.

MIDWEST CHOPPERS 2004 SOFTAIL

Midwest Choppers offers customers a wide variety of custom-built machinery, and this 2004 model is one of the latest entries into the catalog. Built using a softail frame, it rides as good as it looks.

Owner: Rod Getz

The sculpted rear fender adds a flair of fantasy to the tribal flame paint scheme. The sheet metal is designed to hug the rear rubber, although it leaves no room for a passenger.

This stylish and comfortable example has been fitted with an S&S V-twin motor that displaces 124 cubic inches. The shapely, yet truncated, exhaust pipes bark more than they bite, but do bear a certain resemblance to a hungry snake.

APPLETINI

Assembled using a Paul Yaffe frame, this special construction also includes hardware taken from production Harley-Davidson models as well, as several custom builders bits and pieces. The final result looks like everything came from the same place.

Owner: Sound FX Motorcycle Engineering

The flowing lines of the fuel tank are wrapped in a paint scheme of Sour Apple and Grape and accentuate the length of the housing. With an 8-month build time, no efforts were spared when mating all the required hardware into a consistent package.

A total of 103 cubic inches of V-twin power are enclosed within the chrome cases of this mill. Based on the latest Twin Cam B motor from Milwaukee, it takes in fuel through an S&S Super G carburetor and exhales through another component from the house of Paul Yaffe Originals.

BLUTINI

Credit for the frame design on this special construction model goes to West Coast Choppers, but the build and creation was done by the owner in about 6 months. The front forks were purloined from a Harley-Davidson Duece, raked to a 45-degree angle with 4 inches over. A Revtech 100 motor provides the power, and the fumes leave via the Paul Yaffe Originals exhaust.

Owner: Sound FX Motorcycle Engineering

Every inch of sheet metal is coated with a combination of custom mix blue and silver metal flake paint. Placement of the fuel tank flows directly into the frame, creating a seamless, flowing design. Nothing looks like it was added on at the last minute; all was considered before the construction even began.

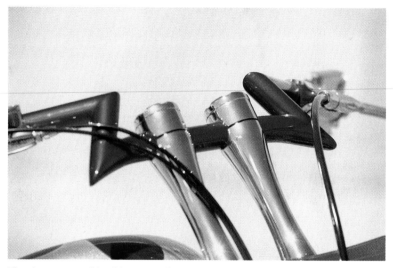

The risers are machined into a gentle, tapered shape, and put the "Z" bars within the rider's reach. The risers are finished off with a set of West Coast Choppers revolver caps. The bars haven't gone without notice, and are also coated with the custom mix blue paint shared with the rest of the bike.

Rims at both ends of the bike are from Performance Machine, and are slathered with chrome. Front- and rear-mounted disc brake systems are also from Performance Machine, and deliver quick, safe stops while still looking great. Metzeler rubber keeps both wheels off the pavement.

SOUND FX
LOADED DICE

A West Coast Choppers CFL frame was used as the basis for this hot rod-themed example. Steering is compliments of another Harley-Davidson Deuce, but the fork is 4 inches over with a 42-degree rake. A layer of black powder coat was applied to the lower sections of the suspension. Black Bike spoke wheels roll at either end of this 1950's throwback.

Owner: Sound FX Motorcycle Engineering

The power plant may look like a vintage Panhead, but looks can be deceiving. The Harley-Davidson cases are packed with a cam and pistons from Headquarters, as are the cylinder heads and ignition. The stubby exhaust system comes from Joker, but produces a serious sound. The cylindrical oil tank is part of the West Coast Chopper frame, and really fits the part of a hot rod chopper.

The forks and risers are held in place using blacked-out triple-trees, and once again the risers are topped off with a set of West Coast Choppers sixgun caps. The virtual lack of chrome on this model enhances the early hot rod theme that characterizes the bike.

The truncated rear fender shares the same satin black paint as the rest of the sheet metal. Hot rod-style pin striping adorns several surfaces on the bike, and the Von Dutch "flying eyeball" adds another touch of 1950's rodding to the overall creation.

SPIRIT CHOPPERS CUSTOM

Joining the fray of custom chopper builders, Spirit Choppers began with this example that was built from the ground up. The rigid frame features a 42-degree rake on the front forks, which are of the springer variety. The palate is borrowed from the Dodge Viper catalog, with Viper Red and Viper Yellow being applied as the base colors. Emerald green pin striping sets the flames apart from the rest of the design.

Owner: Jon Hartsell

The Viper Yellow frame tube can be seen just below the fuel tank. A classic paint job uses colors that are somewhat off the beaten track. The yellow-on-red array is offset by green stripes, helping to create a traditional theme with a modern twist.

This red-and-yellow monster is powered by a 100-cubic-inch motor from RevTech. CCI ignition provides the spark required to fire the big V-twin into life, and a twisted set of pipes from Sampson provide a quick getaway for expelled fumes.

RETRO HONDA

Soon after Honda's introduction of the CB750 Four in 1969, owners began creating choppers propelled by the powerful, smooth motor. This example is a modern day recreation of the 1960's variant. The frame and fuel tank are both handmade for the machine and the motor is taken from a 1977 CB750K model. The springer front fork is another custom-built component on this contemporary version of a 1960's classic.

Owner: Keith Barnett

The rear end lacks any form of suspension, as is typical with most custom-built choppers. The rear wheel is a 16-inch Invader, dipped in chrome. A simple drum brake is responsible for slowing the Honda-powered craft.

The inline four-cylinder motor is all stock within the factory cases. A Dyna ignition provides the required energy to the plugs, and 34mm Mikuni carburetors provide more than adequate breathing. A Fubar exhaust lets the machine exhale as well as it inhales. The blacked-out cylinders and cases are offset by the chromed heads and covers.

PIMP

This creation is the culmination of 5 months of build time and a wide variety of manufacturers components. A Santee rigid frame is teamed up with a front fork by Pro One that's 14 inches over and rides with a 50-degree rake. The sissy bar, brake and shift pedals were all hand crafted by the owner to accessorize the factory-built pieces. The black-and-red color scheme extends all the way to the 80-spoke rims.

Owner: Tim Wookey/Wooks Custom Choppers

The 100-cubic-inch motor comes from Altima, and produces 110 horsepower. The S&S Super G carburetor draws breath through a single, machined velocity stack. A Crane Hi 4 ignition provides the spark, and Eddie Trotta exhaust provides uninterrupted breathing.

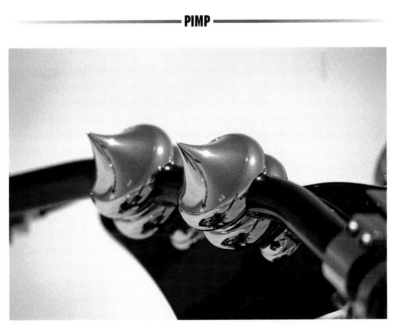

The drag bars are finished in gloss black, as are the risers. Holding the bars in place are these sculpted caps, adding a touch of sparkle to the dark-colored chopper.

The handmade coffin tank was hand crafted in California for the owner. The graphics are completed with a combination of flames and gold leaf, along with the figure that could have been found on a WWII bomber plane's nose.

"BLACK JACK ACE"

Built by Bourget's Bike Works in Arizona, the "Black Jack Ace" is a complete "factory" machine that can easily be assembled to meet custom needs. Powered by a 113-cubic-inch motor from S&S, it shifts through a six-speed transmission by Jim's. The Primo belt drive makes sure all the power reaches the wheel. This edition is done in the chopper mold, complete with a 45-degree rake, but a more conventional chassis is also available.

Owner: Ideal Ride

Adding to the Black Jack's appeal are the Bourget wheels, cut from billet and bathed in chrome. The triple-ace design melds perfectly with the theme of the bike, and the front rim is mated to a single disc brake for confident stopping power.

One of Bourget's many trademark design elements is the tubular rear swingarm. The Black Jack Ace is a softail model, which provides the comfort of rear suspension with the looks of a hardtail design. Another disc brake is used on the rear wheel to intensify the braking power needed to slow the 113-cubic-inch beast.

DRAGO'S 1975 FXE CUSTOM

Not content to ride a common chopper, the owner of this machine took it into his own hands to create a one-of-a-kind machine. The frame has been highly modified to accept the dual-tube front forks, 3-gallon Sportster tank, sissy bar and rear shocks. Based on a 1975 FXE, the motor has also been massaged to reach 101 cubic inches. The paint on the bike matches the owner's personal tattoos.

Owner: Drago's H-D Garage

The parallel downtubes of the handmade front forks are the owner's design and construction. By adding a second set of hydraulic downtubes, the suspension capabilities have been doubled, and the "wow" factor exceeds that figure by far. The triple-trees and front hub also had to be custom-machined to meet with the owner's special demands.

To complement the double down tubes of the front forks, a second set of rear shocks have also been added to this highly modified machine. Both lower and upper mounting positions had to be crafted to mount the dual shocks on each side of the modified frame.

1996 X-TREME HARLEY

Based on a 1996 Harley-Davidson FXWD, this example was built to show what could be accomplished on a smaller budget. Although the rake of the forks are standard, the rear suspension was lowered by 2 inches to change the stance of the machine. A custom-made fuel tank was also mounted to the frame to alter the overall appearance.

Owner: X-Treme Cycle Tech

Adding another custom touch to this low-buck build is the embroidered saddle cover. It is done off-center to mimic the work of a real spider, and provides a nice touch of color to the otherwise blacked-out machine.

Unable to find the perfect exhaust system, X-Treme constructed this unusual upside-down "U" system. Internal baffles force the spent gases to travel in the most efficient manner, and eliminate blowback. The flat black finish makes them stand out from the chrome examples used on other customs.

With the custom-built exhaust, it only seemed right to create a pair of intake pipes for the carburetor. The jet-black church pipes draw oxygen directly into the throat of the carb, and really make a nice addition to the theme of the chopper.

X-TREME "THUGSTER"

X-Treme Cycle Tech has earned a reputation as a builder that breaks all the rules. The "Thugster" is proof of that design principle. The custom-bent frame holds the forks at a 40-degree rake and cradles the 80-cubic-inch Harley motor, too. The fuel tank, control-free handlebars and single clutch/brake lever are additional proof of the builder's abilities.

Owner: X-Treme Cycle Tech

The only control pedal found on the bike is this right foot device. By depressing the pedal halfway you activate the clutch. Push the pedal to the end of its travel to provide braking to the rear wheel. The rear hub was created from a Dayton automotive wheel.

A plush saddle just wouldn't look right on this minimalist chopper, so the rider plants his posterior on this thinly padded pillion instead. The House Of Color metal flake covers every inch of the sheet metal and is accented by the perfect use of pin striping.

X-TREME HONDA REBEL CHOPPER

Wanting to build a chopper for his wife, X-Treme Cycle Tech's owner chose a smaller, lighter machine from Honda as the base. A 1986 Rebel 250 gave its life to become a custom chopper on this build. In typical chopper fashion, the rear suspension was removed and replaced with a rigid strut. A custom-built coffin tank was also created to change the appearance of the once docile machine.

Owner: X-Treme Cycle Tech

Continuing on the chopper theme, the rear fender has been bobbed and sculpted. The dual exhaust terminates in a pair of fishtail tips. The new exhaust makes the 250 motor sound like a Triumph from the 1960s.

Since this was going to be the female rider's first motorcycle, the project needed to begin with something small and light. The Honda Rebel 250 was a perfect candidate for the fabrication. The vertical twin motor provides enough power for in-town and on-the-highway journeys. Going from stock Honda to full-blown custom took about 4 months.

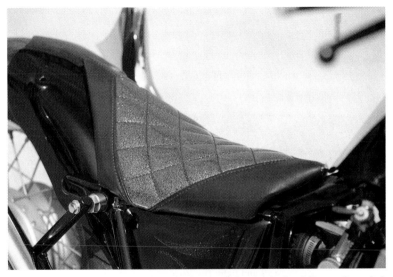

To complete the transformation from stock to cool, the standard saddle was discarded. This new pillion was custom formed, then covered in "boat flake" vinyl. It makes a perfect partner for the black silver flake paint with accenting flames.

X-TREME LOW RIDER

A specific combination of hardware was used to make this chopper long, low and fast. A 96- cubic-inch motor was mounted to the custom frame, and 45-degree rake was applied to the front fork. With fork legs that measured 10 inches over stock, the long and lean appearance was achieved. An 18-inch wheel out back was mated to a 21-inch version up front.

Owner: X-Treme Cycle Tech

The majority of the internal components are from S&S, as well as the carburetor. A matching pair of magnetos deliver plenty of energy to fire the beast. The Samson pipes are wound with heat wrap tape and finished off with anodized fittings for a tidy appearance.

The straight pipes terminate in straight cuts and deliver plenty of sound while providing free breathing. The rear suspension has been replaced with solid struts much like a drag race chopper. The drilled disc rotor delivers the stopping power.

AMERICAN IRONHORSE TRIBUTE BIKE

Built to honor the the owner's late friend, this machine began life as a stock IronHorse model. Over the 6-month build period, almost every major component was switched to something more suitable to the owner. New triple-trees, front forks and fenders changed the looks of the stock bike, while a Screaming Eagle clutch and Martin Brothers shift lever altered the running gear. The paint scheme was also dreamt up for style and memory.

Owner: Roland Ochoa

The solid disc rear wheel hails from American Iron-Horse, as do the brakes. A 240 series rear tire from Metzeler keeps the chrome rim off the pavement. The upswept exhaust pipes were bent by Samson, and as usual there is no rear suspension.

The V-Twin power plant displaces 113 cubic inches, and is largely an S&S affair. An S&S carburetor monitors the flow of fuel, and it's lit by a Power Arc ignition. The jockey shift lever was provided by the Martin Brothers, and the tribal flame contour melds nicely with the flowing checkerboard paint.

The custom sheet metal is treated to a flowing winner's flag color scheme that ends on the rear fender. Built to remember a fallen friend, the dates are also included on the tail end of the metal.

APC HIGH ROLLER

Another model in the 2003 American Performance Cycle catalog is the High Roller. Chassis dimensions provide a 38-degree rake, a 4-inch stretch on the frame, and another 7-inch stretch on the fork tubes. A 240 series rear tire is mounted to a rim that matches the pulleys and sprockets, as well as the front wheel. Braided stainless-steel is used on all cables and lines to provide safety and good looks.

Owner: Windwalker Motorcycles of Naperville

The front forks are smooth and blended, and feature an upside-down layout. The 21-inch, 90 series front tire is stretched around an 80-spoke rim. The Soft Ride suspension on the rear wheel delivers comfort and control.

Rev Tech provides the V-Twin motors to APC, and they can be ordered in any displacement starting at 88 cubic inches. A six-speed transmission is used to keep the motor running in the sweet spot of the rev range.

APC HIGH ROLLER 280

American Performance Cycle, otherwise known as APC, builds a complete line of "stock" custom choppers. Each model comes complete with a lengthy list of features, and those can be complimented with a large variety of options. By combining these variables, the buyer can create a machine to meet his or her specific needs. The High Roller 280 seen here features right-hand drive and a large 280 series rear tire. The 38-degree rake and 7-inch stretch on the fork tubes give the rider an aggressive stance with which to base the rest of the design.

Owner: Windwalkers Motorcycles of Naperville

The base price of every APC machine includes your choice of custom paint. This allows every buyer to have a machine like no other. This vaporous flame job also includes the phantom skulls that are incorporated into the work. The rear fender is part of the Soft Ride suspension, which delivers comfort along with a radical appearance.

With a right-hand drive system, the pulley and belt reside on the opposite side of most bikes. All pulleys, flywheels and rotors on the APC machines are cut to match, but are offered in a variety of styles. The High Roller mates a 280 rear wheel with a wide 130 front for an aggressive look.

GUITAR BIKE

Although the High Roller 280 is a standard model sold by American Performance Cycle, this example has been outfitted with the most extreme dimensions available. The 38-degree rake is matched to fork tubes that carry a 7-inch stretch. An additional 4-inch stretch of the frame provides the radical geometry of the High Roller 280.

Owner: Windwalkers Motorcycles of Naperville

At the heart of this right-hand-drive bike is a 124-cubic-inch monster motor from S&S. While a 280 series rear tire would typically seem like overkill, it's barely enough rubber to keep the bike planted under hard acceleration.

All choppers need a kickstand to hold them up while parked, but this one has gone a step beyond. The fishnet-clad leg is complete with the handcuff ankle bracelet, giving this example a leg up on the competition.

The guitar-themed graphics on this model are a reflection of the owner's love for vintage and collectible instruments. The winding ribbon of guitars and gold leaf can be found on every surface of this radical ride.

BOURGET'S "PYTHON CHOPPER"

Another ride from Bourget's Bike Works is the "Python Chopper." The Python offers the buyer a wide variety of options in a well-designed package. A Bourget exclusive is the jackshaft design and power plants that measure up to 145 cubic inches in displacement. These upside-down front forks are built by Mean Street and feature a 45-degree rake and are 14 inches over.

Owner: Jay Hansen

The tubular and billet tail section is another trademark of a Bourget's machine. Rear tires come in sizes ranging from a 250 series all the way up beyond 300. To keep a neat appearance, Bourget's Python choppers utilize an oil-in-the-frame design that eliminates the need for a separate oil tank. The candy red paint on this example was applied by Deano's and makes a nice companion to the extensive chrome.

Often used on modern sport bikes, the stout upside-down front forks provide both style and handling. The 45-degree rake and 14-inch-over configuration deliver the posture and appearance demanded by today's chopper buyer.

The finely sculpted fuel tank is draped in candy red paint, accented by metal flake tribal graphics. The details in the graphics help to offset the blanket application of the glowing red lacquer.

AMERICAN IRONHORSE TEJAS

American IronHorse has a "factory chopper" catalog that offers the buyer a myriad of options. The Tejas seen here is the first ever built by the firm and carries VIN 001. It was also the first machine on the market to ride on a 240 series rear tire. The 38-degree rake and 6-over forks may seem mild compared to some choppers, but the dimensions suit the Tejas to a T.

Owner: Dave Plote

Although the chassis dimensions may not be remarkable, the original 113-cubic-inch motor has been massaged up to 120 cubes by Ideal Ride for an added dose of power. The enhanced motor blows the expended gases through this graceful two-into-one exhaust system, allowing the bigger motor plenty of breathing capacity.

While many choppers wear paint of a generic nature, the graphics on this example are far more personal. Reflecting the owner's principles of motorcycling in graphic terms lets him ride a personal statement that also shows off his company's corporate badge.

RADICAL RIGID COMBINATION

Dissatisfied with what he could buy through the "standard" chopper stores, the owner of this bike decided to combine some of the most extreme components and create a machine to meet with his own needs. A rigid Daytec frame was raked 54 degrees and matched with a set of Forks By Frank that measured 32 inches over. The matte black finish is complemented by a hint of chrome for a dramatic affect.

Owner: David Buerer

In an effort to keep a consistent design theme, the owner chose a 93-cubic-inch Flatside Shovelhead motor to power his rig. S&S components fill the cases, and the entire package is fired by a Mallory ignition. The owner also custom bent the exhaust pipes to complete the motor.

It should come as no surprise that the rear end is devoid of any suspension. The rigid frame does, however, roll on 60-spoke wheels wrapped with Metzler rubber at both ends. Performance Machine binders do the braking.

2003 AMERICAN IRONHORSE TEXAS CHOPPER

American IronHorse offers a line of models, each catering to a slightly different rider. This 2003 Texas Chopper is one of the more radical chassis. With a 38-degree rake and a 12-over front fork, the stance is high and open. A 240 series rear tire gives the Texas model a big footprint on the open road.

Owner: Ideal Ride

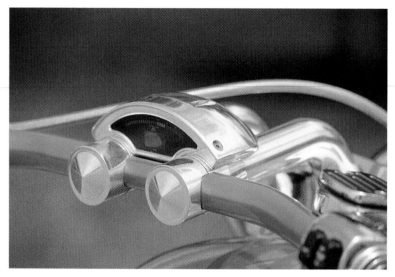

Unlike many of the choppers found on the road, the Texas model comes with electronic instrumentation to keep the rider informed. The majority of choppers being ridden today lack any gauges, forcing the rider to go by the seat of his or her pants.

The Texas Chopper is powered by a 107-cubic-inch motor from S&S. American IronHorse uses its own ignition system to fire the spark plugs, and Crack Pipes is the selected vendor for the exhaust.

An elongated fuel tank holds 4 gallons of the precious commodity, and allows the Texas chopper to travel a fair distance before needing to refuel. Of course, the riding habits of the pilot will raise or lower the mileage greatly.

BOURGET'S RETRO

One of the many choppers created and built by Bourget's Bike Works is this Retro model. The radical appearance is enhanced by a design that ties the frame and bodywork into one integrated component. The fuel tank is an integral part of the chassis, and the gasoline and oil are actually carried in the frame tubes. Unlike other motorcycles, this machine has a fuel tank that cannot be removed. This Retro was sprayed with the patriotic red, white and blue color scheme.

Owner: Ideal Ride

Bourget's Bike Works has made a reputation for using an unusual tubular tail section its trademark. The Retro model takes that design theme to the extreme, and provides the rider with stiff construction and a look like no other. The flag motif does nothing to tone down the visual input of the design.

To keep the 113-cubic-inch motor fed with fossil fuel, a stretched and sculpted fuel tank was applied to the Retro. The angular contours of the sheet metal are also draped in the stars and stripes paint, making an all-American statement.

Steering on the Retro is achieved with the use of this springer front fork. Seated at a rake of 47 degrees, and featuring 18-over fork tubes, the stance is hardly traditional. Dipping the entire assembly in chrome does nothing to hide its extreme dimensions.

MIKE'S CHOPPERS 918 BIG DADDY

Big Mike's Choppers out of Oregon is the source for the 918 Big Daddy model we see here. It appeals to those whose tastes and pocketbooks are a little less exotic. Still a well-made machine, it stays with the basics of chopper design and fabrication.

Owner: Ideal Ride

In keeping with the simplicity of its design, the 918 Big Daddy's bars hold a simple speedometer in position. The bend of the bars, the grips and controls are all fairly standard, adding to the mix and keeping the cost down.

The simplicity of the 918 Big Daddy is reflected in the peanut fuel tank—no wild stretches or contours, just a good place to keep a few gallons of motivation on board. The green metal flake flames make a nice contrast on the gleaming black base color.

A 100-cubic-inch motor from Rev Tech delivers the power to the rear wheel, and the bologna-cut exhaust pipes are straight from the Samson catalog. Sixty-spoke rims are fitted to both ends, and Avon rubber keeps the chrome off the street.

APC SPIRIT S

American Performance Cycle has something for almost every rider, and the 2004 Spirit S is proof of the company's diversity. The Soft Ride chassis features the Blind Axle Swing Arm, and with only a 36-degree rake and 3-inch stretch, the design is more conventional than some others being sold today. The moderate layout provides the buyer with plenty of comfort and style.

Owner: Windwalkers Motorcycles of Naperville

A Rev Tech 100-cubic-inch motor comes standard in the Spirit S, but larger displacement mills can be had with a simple check on the order form. Six-speed transmissions were made standard on all 2004 models from APC in 2004.

A 240 series rear tire is used, and 80-spoke wheels are found at both ends of the 2004 Spirit S. The Blind Axle Swing Arm keeps things neat, while the Soft Ride suspension makes things comfortable.

APC HUSTLER

The 2003 Hustler from APC suits the rider who is looking for a comfortable, yet interesting, chopper to spend the days on. The mild 34-degree rake of the Fat Boy-style front forks delivers plenty of control with a hint of attitude. The 3-inch stretch only adds to the dark side of the Hustler.

Owner: Windwalkers Motorcycles of Naperville

A full-size speedometer resides at the end of the chrome tank panel, along with the rotating ignition switch. As with the rest of the sheet metal, the Hustlers comes with your choice of custom paint.

The nacelle that encompasses the headlight is reminiscent of the Harley-Davidson "Glide" models of the 1950s and 1960s. It makes for a perfect match with the large-diameter, tapered fork legs.

APC features its Blind Axle Swing Arms to hide the typical hardware from cluttering up the look of its machines. The Hustler is built using pulleys, rotors and a wheel that are cut in the same style for a cohesive design throughout.

SUICYCLES COMBINATION HARLEY BOBBER

This flat black machine is the combination of many years of Harley-Davidson parts, as well as many handmade components. The modern Evolution motor is bolted to a Shovelhead transmission, and they both rest in a Panhead frame. The front forks were borrowed from a 1937 Knucklehead. Displacement of the mill was bumped to 89 cubic inches, and it breathes through an S&S Super B carb.

Owner: Suicycles

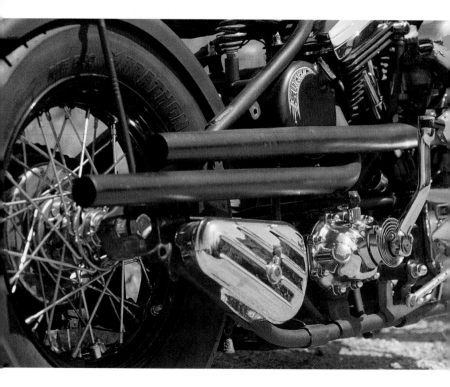

The contemporary motor exhales through a set of handmade straight pipes, finished in the same matte black paint as the rest of this bobber. The kidney-shaped tool kit is from a vintage Harley, and is trimmed in chrome to offset the otherwise all-black motif.

The peanut fuel tank was lifted from a Sportster and now resides just behind the flat drag bars. To monitor distance, rpm and speed, a small computer designed for use on a mountain bike was installed on the bars. The reading device was modified to mate with the front hub, and all fabrication was done by the owner.

The hand shift lever is topped off with an 8-inch ball from a billiard set, and the rectangular battery box is pure vintage Harley. The open primary makes itself obvious without any hint of protective covers.

1955 PANHEAD SPECIAL

This example began its life as a 1955 Panhead in a basket. The owner was born in 1955 and thought it would be fun to build a machine from the same year. with bits and pieces borrowed from friends, the finished machine is considered a collaboration. One long winter was all it took to bolt, weld, paint and polish the parts into one machine.

Owners: Angelo DelRaso, Doug Jurkas, Suicycles

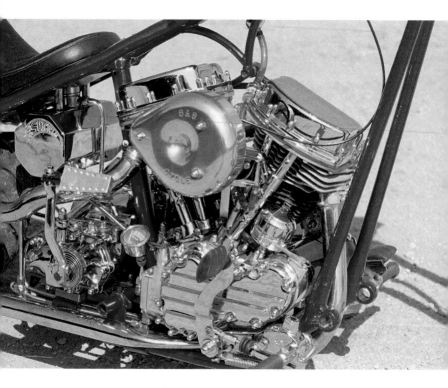

Displacement of the Panhead motor remains at a stock 74 cubic inches, but many of the internals have been updated. The pistons and cam are from S&S, as well as the "L" model side bowl carburetor.

As with many parts on this machine, the origin of each component has become a mystery over the years. The coffin-style fuel tank is as popular a choice today as it was back in the 1960s.

The springer front forks are another common choice among both modern and old-school chopper builders. The ancestry of this set is unrecorded, but it looks great anyway. The chrome finish adds another touch of flash to the project.

HI-PO SHOVELHEAD

Construction of this Shovelhead chopper began in 1974, and has been ongoing ever since. Constant revisions and additions were made as the years rolled by and it has reached its final stages only recently. The builder/owner specializes in high-performance stroker motors, mainly of the Pan and Shovelhead variety. The frame was modified to its current form and the forks measure 4 inches over stock, with a minor rake.

Owner: Dragon's

Of the many hand-built components on this bike, the fuel tank is the most obvious. The angular top and sides are combined with a curved front plate, creating an original form that fits the nature of the chopper.

The 98-cubic-inch power plant now delivers 110 horsepower at the rear wheel—a far cry from the motor's original output. Built by the owner, it includes internals from S&S and Sifton and is fired by a Dyna ignition.

A chopper with this many custom-built pieces would never seem right with a set of factory pipes, so the builder decided to make his own to better match the theme and power of the machine.

JOHNNY LEGEND CUSTOMS MODERN MARVEL

Á veteran motorcycles racer by age 16, the builder of this bike began to design and assemble custom machines in 2001. This recent example and includes a wide variety of the highest-tech gear around. The R.C. Component frame is fitted with air suspension that allows the ride height to be adjusted to meet with conditions.

Owner: Johnny Legend Customs

The most outlandish feature of this machine is the single-sided swingarm from R.C. Components. The drive pulley does double duty as the disc brake, and it gets squeezed from both sides by a four-puck caliper.

One advantage of a single-sided swingarm is the ability to show off the entire wheel on the open side. This R.C. Component rim is encircled by a 250 series tire from Avon.

To complete the range of custom-built bits, the double-layered rear fender is a design original to the owner. Sculpted from steel, it adds the finishing touch to a long list of handmade pieces found on this modern day chopper.

REHABBED HARLEY SHOVELHEAD CUSTOM

After it was delivered to Suicycles as a basket case, it took an entire year to bring this highly modified Shovelhead to life. Most of the original Milwaukee hardware was scrapped and replaced by handmade parts to create a machine to meet with the owner's demanding riding style. The Wide Glide forks have been extended by 12 inches and a mild rake was also applied to the frame.

Owner: Suicycles/Dan Hansen

The generator-equipped Shovelhead motor has been punched out to 98 cubic inches with S&S slugs riding within the cylinder walls. An S&S crank is matched with an Andrews cam to keep everything moving smoothly. The exhaust system is a custom design for this machine.

Perched atop the tapered risers are a set of handmade "Z" bars. The grips are a catalog item, but many other components on the bike were machined to match the drilled-out pattern.

A 2-gallon peanut tank was taken from a Sportster and was finished in a two-tone blue flame paint job. The small tank doesn't provide much riding distance, but gives the bike a chance to rest in between periods of abuse from the owner.

TITAN GECKO

Titan was at the forefront of building "factory" choppers, and this 2002 Gecko model is a perfect example of their craft. Fitted with a 113-cubic-inch V-Twin motor, it goes as good as it looks. The geometry is fairly tame by chopper standards, but provides a more useable ride for daily commutes.

Owner: Windwalkers Motorcycles of Naperville

Multi-layered graphics give the illusion of sheet metal being torn away to reveal the diamond-plate that lies beneath. A choice of custom graphics is part of the appeal.

Performance Machine brake hardware is utilized on both rims, and provides ample stopping power. An actual set of shock absorbers deliver comfort to the rider and passenger. Many of today's choppers are devoid of any suspension at all, making this machine a luxury vehicle.

This Titan is equipped with many features not found on other radical builds. A full range of switches on the bars, and instruments with indicator lights provide the rider with a full range of information.

INDEPENDENCE MOTORCYCLE COMPANY FREEDOM EXPRESS

The Independence Motorcycle Company hails from Tucson, Arizona, and builds a variety of machines. The Freedom Express offers the buyer a nice bundle of gear for a reasonable cost. The 41mm front forks sit at a moderate 38-degree rake, and the fuel tank holds nearly 4 gallons of precious fossil fuel. This combination allows for long, comfortable days in the saddle. Considered the company's flagship model, this example comes complete with an optional powder-coated frame to match the painted sheet metal.

Owner: Windwalkers Motorcycles of Naperville

Power for the Freedom Express comes from the 100-cubic-inch RevTech motor. A 42mm Mikuni carburetor doles out the fuel/air mixture with precision, and the six-speed transmission does the rest.

The chromed handlebars reach back to the rider thanks to gently curved risers. The resulting riding position, combined with the well-padded saddle, delivers comfort and operator-friendly control.

Each 80-spoke wheel is fitted with a four-piston Thunderheart brake caliper and drilled rotor. Gas-charged shocks reside beneath the frame to soften the ride while retaining the hard tail look.

STEVE MCQUEEN'S '47 INDIAN

It's hardly the prettiest machine on these pages, but this "rat" chopper provided the previous owner with anonymity when being ridden in public. This 1947 Indian chopper was owned and ridden by Steve McQueen whenever he wanted a few minutes of peace and solitude. Donning a helmet and sunglasses gave him enough protection from his adoring fans. Stripped of all the excess hardware, it is truly one of the original choppers. The bedroll tied to the sissy bar let the Hollywood star take a rest whenever the mood struck him, and also added to the mystique of the machine.

Owner: National Motorcycle Museum

PRISON CITY CHOPPERS 280 KAPONE

Prison City Choppers builds each of its machines to meet with the buyer's specific needs. This 280 Kapone model rides with an aggressive 46-degree rake and 10-inch-over forks. It took 3 months to build this example. Limetime Green and Tangelo Orange were the chosen hues.

Owner: Prison City Choppers

Wheels and braking hardware come from Euro Components. The 280 rear tire is wrapped with a close-fitting fender that is honed to a point at the rear edge. Right-hand chain drive provides the rear rubber with power, and suspension from Progressive keeps the tire firmly planted.

Motivation for the 280 Kapone is delivered via the 113-cubic-inch motor from S&S. While S&S components fill the cases, a Crane ignition provides the spark. An exhaust from Grumpy's allows for a free-flowing release of spent gases.

CROWN CUSTOM SPECIAL

A wide variety of hardware and tactics were applied to this custom creation. A Bourget rigid frame steers with Progressive forks. They are canted at a 40-degree rake with 6-inch-over tubes. A 113-cubic-inch motor from TP provides the power, and Samson Street Sweeper exhaust lets it breathe. All the pieces took a year to put together.

Owner: Crown Custom Cycle Fabrication/Walter Anderson

Not only is this chopper fast, the graphics package makes it visually stunning. The base colors are Harlequin Green and Purple, with a wild array of illustrations on top of that. The detail and realism of the images make them truly works of art.

In addition to the terrific graphics and hardware, many areas of the frame have been sculpted and smoothed for a seamless appearance. The rear fender strut has been gently blended with the lower frame tubes. The rims are from Weld Wheels, and the brakes herald from JB.

Every surface on this chopper has been treated with a careful application of graphics and color. The eyes painted on the oil tank appear to be three-dimensional and almost follow you around as you view the details on the bike.

CROWN CUSTOM HI-PO CHOPPER

With a motor that was originally built for use on the drag strip, it comes as no surprise that this machine boasts 165 horsepower from 140 cubic inches of displacement. Activating the on-board nitrous oxide injection system easily adds another 50 ponies to the total. Amateur riders need not apply.

Owner: Crown Custom Cycle Fabrication/Bud Dennis

Basic motor functions are monitored by the handlebar-mounted speedometer and tachometer. Additional gauges reside on the left side of the motor to keep the additional power management numbers within sight.

The flames stitched into the saddle seem appropriate. When hitting the button for the "juice" while already running full speed, "hot seat" would be the perfect description for the red pillion.

Even when building a horsepower monster, neatness counts. Every required bit of hardware is mounted securely, and connected with surgical precision on this bike. When running at full bore, having pieces come lose is not part of the plan.

ROLLING THUNDER

Rolling Thunder delivered the frame used to build this red and silver chopper, and no detail was overlooked in the remaining construction. The Softail chassis rides on Progressive shocks in the rear, and Performance Machine was the chosen source for the wheels and brakes at both ends.

Owner: Bane Dimitrijevic

Momentum is provided with the use of the 100-cubic-inch motor from S&S. A Super G carburetor lets the mix in, while a Wicked Brothers exhaust lets it out. The points cover is trimmed with the DD Custom Cycles logo as well.

A set of Sunmyth front forks hold the front wheel in place, and a 38-degree rake is used for stable steering. The sleek front fender provides complete coverage and hugs the front tire for an integrated appearance.

A pair of gauges imported from Germany monitor the key functions of the machine, and House of Kolor was responsible for the candy red and silver flame paint. Only 3 months were required to assemble the entire chopper.

PRISON CITY CHOPPERS 250 DETH ROW

Another model from Prison City Choppers is the 250 Deth Row. The Kapone chassis was chosen because the owner was having trouble finding a chopper that fit his body comfortably. Not only did this model fit his physique, but it was built to meet his riding style as well.

Owner: Prison City Choppers/Dustin Garman

The elongated fuel tank is trimmed in the same black-and-white scheme as the remaining sheet metal. A set of low bars sit atop the curved risers, and fit the owner's dimensions perfectly.

In traditional chopper fashion, the primary of the big motor is open. This one is fitted with an outer panel that makes a perfect billboard for the builder's name.

A 100-cubic-inch motor from RevTech powers the chopper down the road. A Mikuni carb feeds the mill and a shapely two-into-two MGS exhaust does the exhaling.

IRON ECSTASY

Wanting something different from the store-bought choppers on the market, the owner of this bike brought his list of wants to DD Custom Cycles, and 4 months later rode this extreme machine home. Powered by a 113-cubic-inch mill from S&S, the chopper goes as good as it looks. With a 38-degree rake, a 6-inch stretch in the frame and another 14 inches added to the fork tubes, there's nothing common about the dimensions.

Owner: Barry Boches

While the chosen frame geometry is far from subtle, the red-on-red ghost skull paint job certainly is. Depending on the light, the phantom skulls either stand out or disappear into the base color.

DD Custom Cycles' logo is rather distinctive, and finds a home on the point cover of every machine that leaves the shop. The tribal graphics blend perfectly with the "DD" of the corporate badge.

A 250 series rear tire is stretched around a Trident wheel from Performance Machine, and the front rim is cut to match. Rear braking is delivered with a system from PM, and Legend Air suspension allows the rider to custom tailor the ride height to match his riding habits and changing conditions.

CHICAGO CHOPPER WORKS LONGNECK

With a long history of building bikes under his belt, the owner of this bike decided to set the bar higher and create something that really showed off his skills. Using a Chicago Chopper Works frame, complete with a rake of 52 degrees, the builder added a pair of 18-over forks from Redneck. The total length ended up at just over 10 feet. A 93-cubic-inch Panhead motor from Accurate Engineering puts the machine in motion.

Owner: Steve Schaeffer

A standard fuel tank was chosen, but the raised spine down the center was an addition made by the owner. There are very few catalog pieces used that didn't undergo some alteration. The red jockey shift knob lights up at the touch of a button.

Included on the long list of owner-fabricated parts are the foot controls. The handlebars were also crafted for use on this stretched-out custom.

The rear wheel and tire are wrapped with a fender that is also hand made by the owner. The hidden axle mount adds to the clean design and execution of this chopper. The sissy bar was also specifically fabricated by the owner for use on this bike. Black Bike 120-spoke wheels roll at both ends.

VON DUPOR

This chopper was built as a tool to show what the builder's custom bike building company was capable of. It combines the best of all possible worlds and the result shows every bit of the effort it took to construct. A War Eagle 280 chassis was the basis of the craft, and the front forks were actually shortened by 2 inches to mesh more effectively with the 42-degree rake.

Owner: Dave Dupor/DD Custom Cycles

The rear swingarm is a piece of billet artwork. Teamed up with Tricky Air suspension, the system provides a wide variety of riding and parking positions. The Sinister alloy wheels are a product of Pro One, and have been enhanced with anodized red trim. The drive pulley has also been finished in the same red anodizing.

Fuel storage is completed with the Independent unit that has been modified for use on the chopper. The entire bike is finished in candy silver paint and is accented with Von Dutch-style pin striping.

A 124-cubic-inch S&S motor was wedged into the frame and the cylinders are fed through an S&S Super G carburetor. The trumpet velocity stack keeps the flow focused. Crane ignition keeps the fires hot, while the hot gases escape through an upswept set of truncated exhaust tubes.

RIPPER

In the space of only 3 months, DD Custom Cycles was able to assemble this customer-ordered machine. Built around a Diamond Softail frame, the front forks are from Pro One, and sit at a 34 degree rake. Two inches was removed from the length to enhance ride and control. Independent Gas Tank Company provided the fuel retention unit.

Owner: Adam Garvanian

A 100-cubic-inch motor from Rev Tech is fired by a Dyna ignition system and dumps the wasted fumes through an MGS exhaust. Braided stainless lines keep the fluids flowing.

The fat rear tire is mounted to a Performance Machine Villian wheel, as is the front tire. The softail suspension hails from Legend, and delivers comfort you can't see. The rear fender encompasses the rear tire completely and houses a tiny, brilliant taillight.

NIGHTMARE

Another example of a customer-requested, DD Custom Cycles machine is this 2003 chopper. Assembled using a Pro Street chassis, and MW forks, the 40-degree rake and 6-over tubes create a classic chopper profile. A pair of Performance Machine Gatlin wheels are paired up with brakes from the same maker. The rear suspension comes from Progressive.

Owner: DD Custom Cycles/Derf Simes

A 124-cubic-inch motor from TP Engineering provides plenty of power to the softail chassis. A Mikuni HSR 45 carburetor feeds the twin cylinders, while a Dyna ignition burns the mix. A Wicked Brothers exhaust was installed to handle waste removal.

The open-belt primary is fitted with an ornately cut faceplate that allows the color-keyed pulleys to be viewed from the outside. The candy apple red and silver leaf paint can be found on several locations on the sheet metal.

JAILBREAK PANHEAD

Built to look as if it had just escaped from a local penitentiary, this chopper was assembled using a variety of pieces collected from a group of friends. A 1950 Panhead was used as the platform, but little of the original machine remains. A fuel tank from Mustang and Wide Glide front fork make up the control end of the bike. The rear fender support is made from a section of chain welded into a solid form.

Owner: Matt Reed & Friends

A custom-built frame from Dragon's holds the works together and keeps the 86-cubic-inch Panhead motor in place. Dragon's used both S&S and Leinenweber components inside the motor, then bent an exhaust from scratch to complete the build. The oil tank is crafted from diamond plate and adds to the escapee theme.

If you're looking for "bling-bling" you won't find it here. All guts and no glamour were used when building this machine. The unprotected primary drive and oversized dice shift knob are reflective of the chosen design.

A chopper of this nature could have nothing less than a standard pair of "ape hanger" bars up front. The black plastic grips are mounted high in the air, aided by the mid-level risers.

RECLAMATION SPECIAL

Created and built by a body shop owner in Pittsburgh, this machine began life as wrecked Harley. Goldammer components make up most of the assembly, but go together like hand and glove. Air for the suspension is stored in the upper fork tubes and tubes of the chassis. An air cylinder controls the flow, and allows the ride to be adjusted at any time.

Owner: Chuck Liptak

The billet front forks are from Goldammer, and are as functional as they are sleek. Fitted with a complete air suspension system, the rear end can be raised and dropped using air stored in the fork tubes. A Kodlin headlight assembly is cradled between the tubes as well. The fuel tank is from Yaffe, but has been modified to match the contours of the sheet metal.

Internally, the 2002 Twin Cam 88B motor is all stock, but a carb from Carl's Speed Shop and pipes from Hot Match complete the scene. The motor was disassembled, then chromed and polished before being rebuilt. A custom-made intake was required to mate the carb to the motor.

Both fenders and the oil tank surround were crafted by the builder. The single-sided swingarm from RC Components allows the rear wheel, also from RC, to be shown in its best light. House of Kolor paint was combined with gold leaf and graphics, then clear coated.

VON DUTCH CLASSIC

Von Dutch was a legendary artist best known for his pin striping abilities in the 1960's and '70's. His handywork was seen on almost every surface of the hottest custom cars of the time. Employed for 13 years at Bud Ekin's cycle shop in California, he was exposed to several two-wheeled machines. This example was built by Von Dutch in his formative years and is based on a 1959 Triumph Thunderbird. The seaweed flame job is devoid of any pinstripes, but still delivers the right touch of color and style.

Owner: National Motorcycle Museum

Powered by the factory 650cc vertical twin motor, Von Dutch's personal ride was hardly a rocket, but did provide a solid mount for his around-town adventures. The custom paint extends to the frame tubes, and the engine-turned motor mount is a perfect example of his attention to detail.

Mark Keedy photo

J&P/NESS ANNIVERSARY CHOPPER

To help celebrate its 25th year in business, J&P Cycles had a custom machine built for the party. Not just any builder would do for this highly touted occasion, and none other than Arlen Ness was selected to do the build. A Ness Y2K 145 Digger kit was chosen as the basic layout, then modified to meet with J&P Cycle's desires. An S&S 145-cubic-inch motor powers the anniversary bike down the road.

Owner: J&P Cycles

A unique feature of the Ness Y2K 145 chassis is the dual drive system. Most custom machines are content to glide along with either a single belt of chain delivering power to the rear wheel. With 145-cubic inches on tap, an extra drive belt seems appropriate. One-of-a-kind Stacker pipes were installed to do the heavy breathing.

Regardless of which side you view, you'll find a drive belt on duty. The S&S 145 cubic motor makes huge horsepower and torque, and the dual belts do their best to keep things under control. Rear fender struts are a combination of chrome and matching paint to blend in and complement the overall color scheme.

"MISSISSIPPI QUEEN"

This home-built chopper is a result of adding components from several sources, then throwing in a motor and transmission from a 1974 Harley-Davidson. The Jammer frame holds the springer front forks at a 42-degree rake with a 6-inch stretch. The deeply countoured king and queen saddle provides ample comfort for both rider and passenger. The owner built this bike from start to finish in 1 year.

Owner: Tony Zizzo/Zizzo Racing

The plunger frame design is similar to those used on the early BMWs and delivers a modicum of comfort to the rider while saving stress on the chassis itself. The rear spring tubes wear a simple pinstripe to offset the black paint.

The 1200cc Shovelhead motor was purloined from a 1974 Harley. The internal components are all stock Milwaukee hardware, but spark is provided by Dyna and the exhaust is from Cycle Shack.

The peanut fuel tank sits well back from the steering head, allowing space for the display of graphics. The bike's title is borrowed from an album cover using the same name.

NESS-STYLE '75

It has taken many years, but the name Arlen Ness has finally reached household status. His modern machines embody the spirit of the early years with the highest level of technology available. Influenced by his early designs, this 1975 creation was built by the owner and a local shop, then painted by celebrated artist Tom Taylor. It was state-of-the-art for its time.

Owner: J.R. Pedian

The Shovelhead motor exhales through this massive two-into-one exhaust system crafted by Mel Young, but it does little in the noise suppression department. The Airhart rear disc brake is fitted to an Invader steel-spoke wheel—a popular choice for the builders of the period.

A 48mm updraft carburetor from Weber sits atop a custom-built manifold and does a fine job of keeping the Shovelhead motor well fed. The peanut tank forces the rider to stop often for a refill.

PERSONALIZED HARLEY SOFTAIL

Not content with a wide range of store-bought choppers, the owner of this bike decided to mix and match components to create a bike to fit his own needs. A 1999 Harley-Davidson Softail Custom was chosen as the donor bike. The front forks are raked at 45 degrees and fit the owner's desires for looks and handling.

Owner: Kurt Rewerts

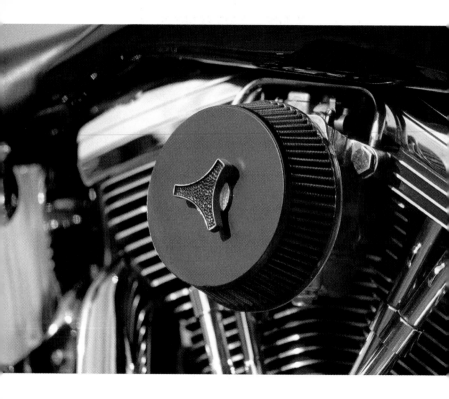

The 80-cubic-inch motor is trimmed with a custom-made air cleaner from X-Treme Cycle Tech, and the krinkle-back finish offsets the chrome motor perfectly.

Avon rubber is teamed up with a set of Vulcan wheels on both ends of the bike. Harley brake hardware handles the slowing and stopping.

Beginning with an off-the-shelf fuel tank, X-Treme applied a few touches to create this unit. The submerged speedometer and twin fuel caps are mated with the deep purple and black graphics for an attractive, subtle effect.

SURGICAL STEED 300 VM APPALOOSA

Surgical Steed Choppers has built bikes in Scottsdale, Arizona, since 1989, and the 300 VM Appaloosa is its latest offering. Among the cadre of features is the massive 30 series rear tire. This new breed of Avon rubber provides a huge footprint and makes good use of the horsepower on tap.

Owner: Windwalkers Motorcycles of Naperville

A choice of 111- or 124-cubic-inch motors from S&S provide the motivation, and the two-into-one exhaust system aids in smooth deliver of the power within. A right-hand drive unit from Baker shifts through the six-speed transmission, giving the rider plenty of gears to work with.

Assisting the rider with a full complement of information, the "heads-up" display in each rearview mirror is a nice addition to many of today's custom-built choppers.

In an effort to deliver both power and comfort, the 300 VM Appaloosa chassis features a Surgical Steed Monoglide rear suspension. Tucked beneath the seat, the chrome spring delivers enough travel to allow longer days in the saddle.

CONFEDERATE 124 HELLCAT

What can be said about a chopper that weighs 500 lbs. and is driven by a 124-cubic-inch motor? The Confederate 124 Hellcat is dripping with the latest high-tech materials and hardware and is definitely one of the most radical machines on the market today.

Owner: Windwalkers Motorcycles of Naperville

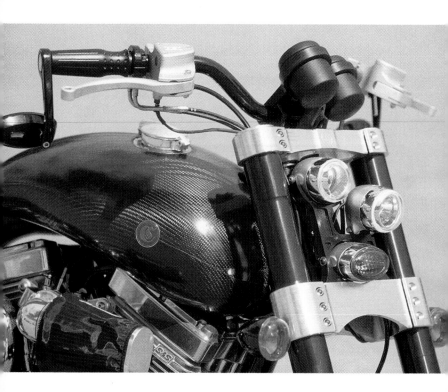

Mounted in front of the carbon fiber fuel tank are a trio of headlights. High, low and wide-low beam project lamps deliver illumination for different conditions and bring another touch of science fiction to the road.

Both front and rear fenders are also formed of carbon fiber and do their part to keep the total weight low. The sleek exhaust blends nicely with the curves of the carbon fiber fender and brings another hint of "space age" to the Hellcat.

With a total of 124 cubic inches of displacement on hand, the Hellcat is not just another pretty face. An output of 130 rear-wheel horsepower means you'll never have to say you're sorry on the street or track. By mounting a five-speed transmission of their own design, the builders were able to change the geometry to better suit the Hellcat's attitude.

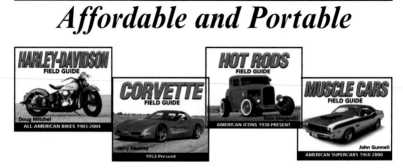